AF375439

Knowing Our Worth

But Is Our Worth Actually What Assets We Have?

Loran Joly

ReEnvision Press

Contents

Preface   v

1. Know Thyself - But in What Ways?   1
2. Know Worth or Know Assets and Liabilities?   3
3. The Greatest Asset?   5
4. The Common Assets of Modern Man?   7
5. Is Complexity a Great Asset?   9
6. Perhaps Our MINDS Contain Our Greatest Assets?   10
7. Mankind Seeks Shortcuts   12
8. If It Ain't Better, Dress It Up With GLOSS?   13
9. What is QUALITY THINKING?   14
10. The Role of Our Words?   15
11. Mankind's View is Shifting to a Cause-and-Effect Mode   17
12. Respect as a Code Word For The Way of Thinking Deterministically About People?   21
13. The Asset of Not Thinking Catastrophically?   23
14. The Asset of Not Using Denials   25
15. The Asset of How to Put Our Ideas Into a Framework?   27
16. The Lesser Assets of Clarity and Seeing What is Most Essential   28
17. Building a Life on Sand Instead of Rock?   30

Preface

The first thing I'll say is that this is book's topic is surely hypothetical, like everything in life.

In fact I may be dreaming that I'm writing this right now, rather than actually writing it while "awake" - and so, even whether we think we are awake or asleep is a hypothesis.

Chapter 1

Know Thyself - But in What Ways?

We have all heard the phrase, "Know Thyself" - as said by Socrates.

And we also hear this phrase, too: "Know Your Worth":

So, we might consider this video:

"This Story Will Help You Understand YOUR WORTH (The Story of The Old Watch)":

https://youtu.be/BQcp1ZNWgTs?si=TxQGrvEnlLCLvJw7

* * *

But isn't "Beauty in the Eye of the Beholder"?

Some like the sport of football, say, and others like the sport of golf, and yet others, the "sport" of chess....

Or say, some enjoy a glass of wine; others, beer; still others, whiskey.

And then, there are those who prefer lemonade or water....

Loran Joly

* * *

And so, is there something else to take a look at, other than saying that our Worth is Relative - Relative to the Observer - to Whatever "Floats Their Boat"?

Chapter 2

Know Worth or Know Assets and Liabilities?

Is there such as think as Truth? Objective Truth?

Or, call it *"Intrinsic* Worth"? A rather murky term, "intrinsic"?

Or, say,

Intrinsic ASSETS?

Or, for short, simply ASSETS - and in this sense, an ASPECT of MATTER or IDEA that is of USEFULNESS to Most Anyone on this Planet?

* * *

But then, what good is an Asset, if it is OVERSHADOWED by a Toxic LIABILITY that is too overpowering for the Asset to be desired, to be used?

Isn't it exactly like picking up a drug at the pharmacy, wherein one wants a drug that has mostly positive benefits and few side effects?

Or else one is going to scratch one's head and wonder whether it's worth it.

Same thing if one is a heroin - utilizer, and obtains cheap heroin - but which has been cut a number of ways and is very toxic to one's body, thus, while at the same time delivering bene-fits, at the same time.

Chapter 3

The Greatest Asset?

Now Brian Tracy, the marketing master and motivational speaker, also urges us to identify our assets:

In a video, he refers to these as "Unique Selling Propositions":

"4 Principles of Marketing Strategy | Brian Tracy":

https://youtu.be/hZLMv5aexto?si=5S3lDZrIXxiKyMiR

And in religious circles, there is an attempt made to simply what some consider the Greatest of Assets in terms of words such as Love:

"Though I speak with the tongues of men and of angels, but have not love, I have become sounding brass or a clanging cymbal."

https://www.biblegateway.com/verse/en/1%20Corinthians%2013%3A1

I am not trying to market one viewpoint or another, simply offering different views on what we consider a great asset....

So indeed, one might ponder whether there are any Unique Selling Propositions, ultimately, other than the concepts involved what makes for the best in human relations: for consider the book "How to Win Friends and Influence People", by Dale Carnegie ....

Chapter 4

The Common Assets of Modern Man?

Now, some people would say that our worth is best measured in our bank account holdings.

Or our possessions, of a matter-based nature.

Noting that I said Matter, not Ideas or Tools of the Mind, including our WORDS.

* * *

Yet others would say our Worth - or our Great Assets - are in what we can trade in terms of our body....

In other words, the asset of making someone else feel Great Pleasure, physically, from "interacting" with our body, vs. our Words, our Core Concepts, and our Commitments or Lines Drawn in the Sand....

In similar fashion to "interacting" with a chemical drug....

Indeed, might we consider sex a form of Crack Cocaine?

And too, a form of "ego"-boosting? (Of self-esteem boosting).

And a tool, even, to boast of our prowess?

Or to put some Sex Object on display, thus, as a Trophy Spouse, like an Ornament in a home - on the coffee table, even, of life?

Chapter 5

Is Complexity a Great Asset?

Yet others would say that it what is intrinsically of high worth is whatever is complex.

But then I would ask: what about the complexities of the computer Deep Blue, which played chess?

"Deep Blue versus Garry Kasparov":

https://en.wikipedia.org/wiki/Deep_Blue_versus_Garry_Kas parov#:~:text=Deep%20Blue%20versus%20Garry%20Kas-parov%20was%20a%20pair%20of%20six,York%20City%20by%203%C2%B

Or robots, for that matter?

Noting, by the way, that our pets are perhaps less complex, by far, than a human being, and yet many prefer our pets to most humans!

Chapter 6

Perhaps Our MINDS Contain Our Greatest Assets?

So, might the Greatest of Assets, to be what is in the Contents of our MINDS?

Our Brains, thus?

Not our Bank Account or Storehouses of Objects, or our Bodies?

* * *

Indeed, this is talked of by Napoleon Hill in "Think and Grow Rich".

The book was not entitled "Get Rich and You'll Be Happiest"; nor, "Get a Great Body and Make Sure to Offer It, and You'll Be Happiest....."

Or, "Get a Great Education, but Not a Great Mind, and You'll Be Happiest....."

* * *

Maybe this is what someone was getting at when they said to me, when I was twenty-one, "Think more for yourself"!

And ten years ago, when someone I knew, was saying, of a group, "They have Bought the Koolaid"....

* * *

For what good is developing Great Logic Skills, alone?

Or, to be able to Handle Complexity well, in and of itself?

Or, too, to be able to remember everything, by having great review strategies?

Or to know a lot of disparate facts, perhaps called "FACTOIDS"?

For, any iPhone camera can take a picture of any number of pages of an encyclopedia, containing lots of Factoids and concepts....

And we can even throw in a conventional Religious Perspective: but is this an end-all?

For, what good is it to Simply Be able to think very logically or very complexly - because computers can do that.

Or too, what good to be able to review very well and efficiently: because an iPhone can do the equivalent as per taking pictures of an encyclopedia - and in short order.

Chapter 7

Mankind Seeks Shortcuts

And so, given all of the above, perhaps today's Modern World has a new spin to the relative ineffectiveness of many so-called Great Assets - often based, arguably, upon SHORTCUTS - call it the Short-Term-Expediency Approach;

or the There is a Free Lunch Concept....

And trying to address, at the same time, a certain sense of hopelessness, too, as per the phrase,

"What has been will be again, what has been done will be done again; there is nothing new under the sun." New International Version

Chapter 8

If It Ain't Better, Dress It Up With GLOSS?

So, maybe Modern Man often turns to GLOSS?

If it is not Greater than Of Old, then, make it GLOSSY!

In other words,

"If we can't make it BETTER, then, at least, make it UNAS-SAILABLE"!

"Beyond Criticism!:"

In other words, make it TYPO-FREE, GRAMMAR-CORRECT, and in 1,000,000k Definition.

DUST it EVERY FIVE MINUTES,

And PUT IT through the CAR WASH every HOUR, too.....

Chapter 9

What is QUALITY THINKING?

And so, what of the MIND, as a GREAT ASSET?
Or of the phrase, THINK and GROW RICH?
Or, mbasically,
"DO QUALITY THINKING"?

* * *

Well, <u>*WHAT MAKES*</u> for "THE BEST THINKING", anyway?

Is it Whatever is MOST "CREATIVE"?

(How do we even define "creative"?)

Is it the GATHERING of the MOST DATA, and then MAKING the BEST SYNTHESIS?

Is it "Thinking Outside of the Box", whatever that might mean?

Chapter 10

The Role of Our Words?

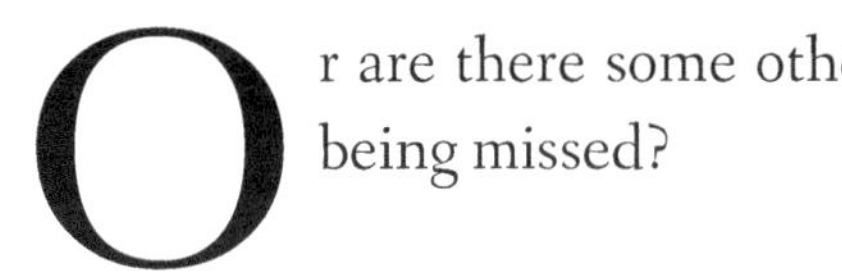

r are there some other CORE CONCEPTS so often being missed?

For instance, we often hear,

OUR WORDS are VERY IMPORTANT.

And, "YOU CAN'T TAKE BACK your WORDS - if the words are TOXIC ones...."

And, "PICK the BEST WORDS"....

And thus, "DON'T STICK YOUR FOOT - don't Stick your BAD WORDS - IN YOUR MOUTH"!

LEST one get lots of BLOWBACK?

Lest one thus be SPITTING in the WIND, and it FLY BACK in one's FACE?

* * *

Now, my thinking has been evolving in this direction:

That it is not enough to say, "Pick Better Words":

For WHAT IF such DON'T EXIST, any more than saying, two hundred years ago, PICK the BEST VACCINE for this or that Disease?

Or, PICK the BEST COMPUTER to SOLVE GETTING to the MOON, when computers DIDN'T EXIST, either, two hundred years ago?

Perhaps this is why The West is said to be so Logic-based, and the East, to have a different orientation of thinking?

Or so it was, until recently?

And too, why the Eastern Philosophers or Religionists had said, "THINK LESS"?

And use MORE INTUITION:

In other words, THINK WITHOUT the USE of TOXIC WORDS, and this then ENTAILING use of INTUITION-based thinking, BECAUSE NON-Toxic words DON'T YET EXIST?

The phrase comes to mind, used here in the West, of course, "If you don't have something POSITIVE to say, then SAY NOTHING at ALL?

Chapter 11

Mankind's View is Shifting to a Cause-and-Effect Mode

So why is it, then, that our WORDS are, in my view, SO PROBLEMATIC, and thus, we - as humans, have SUCH a LAG, SUCH a GAP, between our TECHNO-LOGICAL advances, vs our PEOPLE-area advances?

* * *

I'm just going to say very briefly that I believe Mankind is in a *Great Shift*, from viewing things in a free will fashion to a deterministic fashion, when it comes to PEOPLE:

In other words, that with People, not just Objects, that nothing happens by wishful thinking or spontaneous combustion; rather, that there is the Rule of Cause and Effect for everything, even in the lives of People.

· · ·

And that while such may mean possible despair in the initial stages, for some, don't we also want to Know The Truth?

Indeed, perhaps even two thousand years ago, this was being addressed:

Wasn't it Jesus, indeed, who said,

"And ye shall know the truth, and the truth shall make you free."

John 8:32, KJV

Noting that I am not of a particular faith, but I do bring this Christian scripture up.

* * *

So, why wouldn't Truth include *the Truth about Determinism* as applied to people, not just objects?

For indeed, given Mathematical and Scientific Advances, we have been thinking more and more in terms of CAUSE and EFFECT, in MORE and MORE AREAS of Reality:

INDEED, when it urged upon us to *BE MORE SCIENTIFIC*, are we perhaps actually talking, not, to RUN more EXPERIMENTS and such, but instead, to THINK MORE in terms of DETERMINISM and LESS and LESS in FREE WILL terms?

And not just in the area of OBJECTS, but PEOPLE, too?

* * *

For consider GURDJIEFF the philosopher-religionist, who considered MANKIND to be a biological machine:

"Mr. Gurdjieff says we are "images of God." He also says we are "machines." How could we be both images of God and machines? How to understand this? The gulf between the two is so immeasurable the contradiction seems unresolvable."

https://gurdjiefflegacy.org/40articles/machines-son-of-god.htm

Next, consider Piotr Ouspensky, who spent much time working with Gurdjieff, noting that that Ouspensky was both a philosopher and a *Mathematician:*

"PETER OUSPENSKY
 20TH CENTURY MATHEMATICIAN &
PHILOSOPHER"

"Piotr Demianovich Ouspensky (March 4, 1878–October 2, 1947) was a Russian philosopher who rejected the science and psychology of his time under the strong suspicion that there had to exist superior systems of thought. In his youth, he studied mysticism and esotericism and traveled extensively in search of ancient wisdom, sensing that past ages knew more than his present one. "I felt that there was a dead wall everywhere," he commented in one of his early biographical notes. "I used to say at that time that professors were killing science in the same way as priests were killing religion.""

https://ggurdjieff.com/ouspensky/

"Ouspensky's lectures in London were attended by such literary figures as Aldous Huxley, T. S. Eliot, Gerald Heard and other writers, journalists and doctors. His influence on the literary scene of the 1920s and 1930s as well as on the Russian avant-garde was immense but still very little known.[20] It was said of Ouspensky that, though nonreligious, he had one prayer: not to become famous during his lifetime."
https://en.wikipedia.org/wiki/P._D._Ouspensky

* * *

Indeed, Bertrand Russell was also another example of a philosopher and Mathematician:

And too, Einstein, who said, "God Does Not Play Dice With the Universe":

Indeed, one book of interest,on Einstein's religion, is:

"Einstein's God: A Way of Being Spiritual Without the Supernatural", by Todd Macalister
https://a.co/d/5vBQrzw

Chapter 12

Respect as a Code Word For The Way of Thinking Deterministically About People?

Now, if we are to discuss Mankind in terms of Deterministic Words, my supposition is that this PLAYS OUT, in what we mean, when we say, "Be RESPECTFUL", or, too, "DON'T be MEAN with One's Words"....

But a big problem being, that EVEN IF we INVENT our OWN *DETERMINISTIC* SET of words for PEOPLE, this DOESN'T MEAN that ANYONE ELSE *KNOWS* THESE words, these NEOLOGISMS, in essence, and so, we are SPEAKING "GREEK", to others, or are thus a TOWER of BABBLE;

And WHEN UNDER PRESSURES of TIME and or EMOTIONAL STRESS, we may well TURN to EXISTING FREE-WILL People words - DISRESPECT-based words, even if we have a set of Deterministic words, thus, and have such words fly back in our face....

· · ·

21

As mentioned - in example after example - in the book "How to Win Friends and Influence People".

(Where it is mentioned, in one section, that Abraham Lincoln was once challenged to a duel....)

Chapter 13

The Asset of Not Thinking Catastrophically?

Now, a second GREAT ASSET, I believe, is to PURGE as many CATASTROPHE words from our DICTIONARY and even our HEARING....

As Chris Do may have meant when he once said, "DE-NEUTER" certain words....

De-neuter those words that are CATASTROPHE words.

* * *

I'll just give one example of what I term a CATASTROPHE - word, and leave it at that, for now:

If we hear on the news that someone so was "murdered" by such and such a person, we may be scared:

But when did you ever hear someone say that so-and-so was "murdered" by a heart attack or cancer?

And we never hear anyone say that our "Telomere's have "murdered" us, either:

We simply say that some people die of "old age"...

Here is a short video on this:
"How telomere shortening affects aging":
https://youtu.be/pluI6SOd-_I
And so, the very word we use in how we die, making a CATA-STROPHE out of dying, or not.

Indeed, if one were to discuss things in terms of Psychiatry, or "disorders" - and I say, IF, we might even consider some words from Dr. Aaron Beck, in terms of Cognitive Therapy:
"The Role of Catastrophizing across Psychiatric Disorders"
https://youtu.be/8_9a2v5X6C4

* * *

And all I can say, too, is, *"IF IT BLEEDS, it READS"*.

OR, thus, If it HURTS to HEAR the so-called Catastrophe-Word or Catastrophe-Phrase, it will CAUSE us to want to focus more and more upon it:

Followed by, of course, the going out and BUYING things or DOING things, to make us feel better, via RETAIL THERAPY....

Chapter 14

The Asset of Not Using Denials

Next, What DENIALS are we using?

And perhaps, the use of few or no Denials, could be termed another GREAT ASSET - of the MIND?

Now, some would refer to these with the unpalatable term of "Delusions" or Being "Insane" or "Mad"; others will refer to them as log jams (Florence Scovel Shinn, https://en.wikipedia.org/wiki/Florence_Scovel_Shinn); and yet others would refer to them as limiting beliefs.

Chris Do refers to them as Lies We Tell Ourselves....

Yet others refer to certain sets of denials - if commonplace - as "*mass* delusions".

Noting that perhaps, the Denial of Determinism, as playing out, then, in use of free will based words, and in turn, disrespect, has the most dire consequences....

And thus, some turning to either NON-VERBAL - based "influencing", or finally, by SAYING NOTHING AT ALL - or, too, isolating, to avoid having to encounter what would need addressing with words.

Or by interacting with pets, which in turn is not word-based?

Or through interacting and communicating with Art - a non-word-based form of thought?

* * *

Now, indeed, aren't there perhaps two kingpin denials we so often engage in?

The DENIAL of DETERMINISM when it comes to PEOPLE?

Especially as found in our words we used "off the shelf", in other words, the words in our Dictionaries?

And secondly, the DENIAL that PEOPLE DIFFER, in what is referred to as CHARACTER?

One might take a look at some of the ideas of Robert Greene, for instance:

"The Most Crucial Step in Judging Someone is to Determine Their Character" Robert Greene"

https://youtu.be/NLVNjVpo9FE

Chapter 15

The Asset of How to Put Our Ideas Into a Framework?

Yet more, now - WHAT do we <u>DO</u> with WHAT we OBSERVE, and LEARN, in general?

Is the person who is most skilled at arranging their ideas, also a highly assetted person?

* * *

Put another way, HOW do we PUT all of this DATA into a FRAMEWORK?

Chapter 16

*The Lesser Assets of Clarity and
Seeing What is Most Essential*

Now if I had to mention two more factors of lesser importance, I would say these:

Clarity is critical to making great progress:

Brian Tracy has talked of Clarity - and in his view, Clarity is the greatest of the "7 C's in success;

"The 7 C's to Success with Brian Tracy":

https://youtu.be/FfohcP_zBkQ?si=Td95IdHhucNpYCG6

* * *

Finally, there is a need to be able to see what is most important, and leave the rest behind:

To avoid DATA SMOGGING, in other words,

Or thus, to be able to SEE the FOREST for the TREES.

As Henry David Thoreau sought to do when he went to Walden Pond for two years:

. . .

"In 1845 Thoreau built a small hut on the shore of Walden Pond, near Concord, where he lived in solitude for 2 yrs. It was his experiment in simple, grounded living which, he hoped, would enable him to gain some insight into the primary realities of life. His writing during this time was later published as a book entitled:' Walden ' which encapsulated his feelings on nature, simple right living and the need for solitude. The work offered up profound spiritual insights and wisdom – later becoming recognized as a ' high water mark ' in American literature."

"Thoreau's Experiment with the Simple Life"

By Michael Lewin:

http://www.michaellewin.org/articles/simplicity/thoreaus-experiment/

Chapter 17

Building a Life on Sand Instead of Rock?

S o, to recap:
We have heard the phrase,
"Don't build your house upon the sand":
Might this mean, in practical terms, the matters of "Don't be hurtful by speaking with People-words which are disrespectful, and in turn, thus, words that are based upon Free Will?

And secondly, Don't use words that cause ourselves to Catastrophize?

And thirdly, don't Deny core aspects of Reality?

* * *

So, whether or not one holds stock, these days, in what religious scriptures may say, to any extent at all, these topics have surely been talked of for eons:

Indeed a set of ideas in Christianity verses talk along these lines, I think:

"Therefore whosoever heareth these sayings of mine, and doeth them, I will liken him unto a wise man, which built his house upon a rock:

And the rain descended, and the floods came, and the winds blew, and beat upon that house; and it fell not: for it was founded upon a rock."

Matthew 7:24-25

So, the matter of clarity and data smog are perhaps more minor issues in comparison to disrespect, say.

And so, this perhaps being why some really enjoy reading people such as Ralph Waldo Emerson, or reading poetry, while others say it is too difficult to understand, and not worth the effort, thus: